MYSTERIOUS PYRAMIDS

Ziggurat *of* Ur: *Pyramid of Ancient Mesopotamia*

Murray "Oak" Tapeta

A Crabtree Crown Book

Crabtree Publishing
crabtreebooks.com

Teaching Tips for Caregivers:

You can help your child learn by encouraging them to read widely, both as a leisure activity and as a way of satisfying their curiosity about the world. Reading helps build a strong foundation in language and literacy skills that will help your child succeed in school. This high-interest book will appeal to all readers in intermediate and middle school grades.

Use the following suggestions to help your child grow as a reader.

- Encourage them to read independently at home.
- Encourage them to practice reading aloud.
- Encourage activities that require reading.
- Establish a regular reading time.
- Have your child ask and answer questions about what they read.

Teaching Tips for Teachers:

Engage students throughout the reading process by asking questions like these.

Before Reading

- Ask, "What do you already know about this topic?"
- Ask, "What do you want to learn about this topic?"

During Reading

- Ask, "What is the author trying to teach you?"
- Ask, "How is this like something you have read or seen before?"
- Ask, "How do the text features (headings, index, etc.) help you understand the topic?"

After Reading

- Ask, "What interesting or fun fact did you learn about the Ziggurat of Ur?"
- Ask, "What questions do you still have about this pyramid? How could you find the answers?"

TABLE OF CONTENTS

A PUZZLE FROM THE PAST

The world is full of mysterious places that hold the secrets of lost **civilizations**. Ancient ruins are like snapshots in time. They provide us with important clues about what life was like long, long ago.

Pyramids usually served as grand burial chambers for royalty or as temples for religious ceremonies or both. These structures exist in various forms around the world, built by civilizations that had little or no contact with one another.

*Ziggurats are pyramid-like structures built by the ancient Mesopotamian people. Instead of flat walls, they have several **terraced** levels. No chambers are found inside. Staircases led to temples at the top used for religious worship.*

A Mesopotamian lion hunt, carved into an ancient wall.

PYRAMID STYLES

The word *ziggurat* means "to build high" in the ancient Babylonian language. The Ziggurat of Ur is a step pyramid that was constructed using millions of sun-baked, mud bricks. Ziggurats were temples made of two to seven **tiers**, or layers, each level made somewhat smaller than the one below. On top of the highest tier was a shrine dedicated to a god.

The outside of each tier was glazed a different color: red to represent the underworld, black to represent the earth, blue to represent the sky, and gold to represent the sun.

Tikal - Step pyramid

Ziggurat of Ur - Step pyramid

- 2600 BCE — Giza
- 2500 BCE
- 2100 BCE — Ziggurat of Ur
- 2000 BCE
- 900 BCE — Tikal
- 259 BCE — Qin Emperor

Giza - True pyramid

Teotihuacán - Talud-tablero pyramid

Borobudur - Step pyramid

Qin Emperor - Buried flat-topped, step pyramid

BUILT TO IMPRESS!

Why did so many different ancient cultures build similar towering shapes? Relying on the forces of nature, ancient builders learned that the taller you build, the bigger you had to make the base. This helped distribute the weight more toward the bottom so a very tall structure would not topple over.

210 BCE

100 CE

Teotihuacán

450 CE

778 CE

Borobudur

850 CE

900 CE

THE ANCIENT SUMERIANS

The area now known as the country of Iraq was once called Mesopotamia. The word comes from a Greek phrase meaning "land between the rivers." People settled in southern Mesopotamia around 3500 BCE, in a region that became known as Sumer. The Sumerians established the first cities along the Tigris and Euphrates.

Soon, the cities grew into larger areas called city-states, which included neighboring towns, farmlands, and palm groves. Kings ruled each city-state and often tried to take over other kings' territories.

This wooden panel, made with shells and a stone called ***lapis lazuli****, depicts life in the ancient Sumerian kingdom, including a royal banquet and servants carrying gifts of livestock and fish to the king.*

Ancient Inventors

Sumerians made discoveries in medicine, science, and mathematics that are still important today. They built ships and invented the wheeled cart, the potter's wheel, and other tools. Sumerians also developed a counting system, a calendar, and the first form of writing, called **cuneiform**. Symbols and patterns were made by pressing a reed with a wedge-shaped tip into clay.

SECRETS IN THE SAND

In 1850, British **archaeologist** William Loftus was exploring the Arabian desert. He discovered bricks buried in the sand and took them back to England. Experts there determined that they were from the ancient city of Ur in the time of Mesopotamia. Another British archeologist, John George Taylor, led a team to Iraq and began to **excavate** the site. They found massive mounds in the desert. The mounds were in irregular shapes, suggesting that they were more than just natural hills.

Soon the crew uncovered part of a giant, pyramid-like structure. Work on the site continued for many years with different teams of archeologists. From 1922 to 1934, Sir Leonard Woolley led a crew of British and American archaeologists who removed dirt and sand to finally expose the ruins of the magnificent Ziggurat of Ur.

Ur became a leading Sumerian city by 2500 BCE. In fact, it may have been the largest city in the world from 2030 to 1980 BCE. Historians think about 40,000 people lived in Ur, with as many as 90,000 more in the surrounding area. Winding streets lined with homes, stores, and markets were protected from invaders by walls that surrounded the city. Temples, ziggurats, storerooms, and a "house of tablets," where laws and records **inscribed** on clay tablets were kept, stood at the city's center.

The city depended on **irrigation** from the nearby Euphrates and Tigris rivers. At the height of Ur's strength, its land was fertile and great for farming. Over time, the rivers changed course. The land dried up and became more desert-like. By 530 BCE, Ur was mostly abandoned. Its buildings and monuments, including the great ziggurat, were buried in sand. The once-great city was lost to time.

Most Sumerians farmed, fished, raised livestock, and harvested date palms.

Euphrates River

MONUMENT TO THE MOON

Historians determined that work began on the Ziggurat of Ur around 2100 BCE. The construction was ordered by King Ur-Nammu. Many of the bricks that cover the structure are stamped with his name. However, he did not live to see it completed. The original ziggurat took 10 to 30 years to build. It was completed under his son Shulgi.

Millions of bricks were used to build the massive, four-sided structure. The walls were made from mud and reeds pressed into molds and dried in the sun. Each brick was 11.5 x 11.5 x 2.75 inches (29 x 29 x 7 cm) and weighed up to 33 pounds (15 kilograms).

Originally, the ziggurat had three tiers and three tall staircases. A temple sat on top. Experts believe that the temple was used to worship the moon god Nanna. The temple did not survive, but there is evidence that bricks used to make the temple were colored blue.

Foundation statue of Ur-Nammu

The structure's rectangular base is 210 feet by 150 feet (64 x 46 meters). In ancient times, the Ziggurat of Ur was probably 70 to 100 feet (21 to 30 meters) tall.

CITY CENTER

The towering Ziggurat of Ur stood in the center of the city inside a walled area. It probably served a number of purposes. Some of its uses were practical. It is likely that gardens were planted on the terraces. Farmers and **merchants** may have brought goods to the site for trading. It may have stored crops. People might have come to the central location to pick up their share of food.

Other uses for the ziggurat were spiritual. Some areas might have been used for religious rituals, even human sacrifice. The temple at the top was used for worship.

The Ziggurat of Ur is built like a compass. Each of its four corners points directly to one of the four directions: north, south, east, and west.

TOMBS OF TREASURES

Unlike other ancient pyramids, the Ziggurat of Ur did not contain priceless treasures or **artifacts**. No important rulers were buried inside. However, archaeologists did uncover thousands of graves a short distance away that contained both. Skeletons and other clues in the larger burial sites suggest these people were members of royal families as well as other leaders. Many of these tombs contained valuable objects. The area has come to be known as the Royal Cemetery of Ur.

Near the largest tombs, skeletons were found in mass graves. They are believed to be the remains of servants. It was once thought that they volunteered to drink poison and join their leaders in death. New evidence suggests that they were violently murdered as sacrifices.

WHO'S WHO?

Sumerians developed cylinder seals to sign documents and mark personal property. Cylinder seals were long, narrow stones with patterns carved into them. They left a distinctive pattern when rolled over clay. The discovery of these seals have helped archaeologists identify ancient remains.

Queen Puabi's headdress

One of the most fascinating tombs they discovered belongs to Queen Puabi. The tomb was filled with **ornate** objects made of gold, stone, and clay. Two other people, likely her attendants, were buried with the queen. Queen Puabi's skeleton wore a headdress of gold leaves and strands of lapis lazuli and **carnelian** beads. Elaborate necklaces and a large pair of crescent-shaped earrings were also on the body. Every finger on the queen's hands was decorated with a ring made of precious materials.

lapis lazuli beads

Puabi's remains were the only ones discovered that were clearly identified as royal. A gold pin on her burial garment bore the seal with her name in cuneiform along with the word *eresh*, which means queen. No one is certain if she was the wife of a king or ruled as queen on her own. The burial chamber above her may also have belonged to her. It contained the skeletons of 21 people, likely attendants, as well as highly decorated items to use in the **afterlife** such as a chariot, a harp, and items for grooming.

carnelian beads

Necklace of gold

TIME AND CHANGE

The Ziggurat of Ur changed over time. It was an important building for about 2,000 years until it fell into disrepair. In the sixth century BCE, King Nabonidus of Babylon ordered a **restoration** of the ziggurat. By this time, what the original building looked like was long forgotten. Nabonidus added four tiers, making the structure seven levels high. When Loftus excavated the ruin 2400 years later in the 1850s, only the original bottom tier and two reconstructed tiers survived.

In 1792 BCE, King Hammurabi made the city of Babylon the capital of his empire. He ordered the construction of temples, city walls, public buildings, and canals. Hammurabi is best remembered for developing a code of law that focused more on punishing wrong-doers than ***compensating*** *victims.*

Ruins of the city of Babylon

KING NABONIDUS

In 614 BCE, a series of Babylonian kings fought one another for control of Mesopotamia. The city of Babylon's last king was named Nabonidus. The priests of Babylon turned against him when he ignored festivals that honored Marduk, the king of the gods. Nabonidus had the Ziggurat of Ur restored to honor the moon god instead. The priests of Babylon welcomed the invasion of the Persians, ending Nabonidus's short reign.

RESTORATION OR DESTRUCTION?

Modern-day restorations of historical ruins usually try to rebuild using the same or similar processes and materials used to make the original structure. In the 1980s, Saddam Hussein was the president of Iraq. He ordered the restoration of the ziggurat's massive foundation and stairs. No attempt was made to rebuild the ziggurat using ancient techniques. Modern bricks were used and Saddam had his own name stamped into the bricks. The new **facade** covered most of the original ruins from view. Many historians criticized the restoration as being historically inaccurate.

In 1991, during the Persian Gulf War, Saddam had his air force park their MiG fighter jets near the structure. He believed that American bombers would be too afraid of damaging the ancient site to strike the planes. Unfortunately, the Ziggurat of Ur did get damaged during the Persian Gulf War. It was shaken by explosions and peppered with over 400 bullet holes.

MiG fighter jet

The reconstructed Ishtar Gate, one of eight gates in Babylon

A New Babylon

Saddam wanted to tie his own leadership to ancient Mesopotamian leaders known for their strength and the landmarks they left behind. In addition to rebuilding the Ziggurat of Ur, he had the entire ancient city of Babylon reconstructed. King Nebuchadnezzar II, who ruled from 605 to 562 BCE, built the original city of Babylon. It had an enormous palace protected by the equally large Ishtar Gate. He also built the Hanging Gardens of Babylon, one of the seven wonders of the ancient world, on the ledges of a ziggurat.

UR WELCOME

Today, more than 4,000 years after it was first built, the Ziggurat of Ur is open for visitors to explore. People can also tour the ruins of Ur and the Royal Cemetery. The site is fragile. It's not always possible to climb to the top of the ziggurat. Even so, people come to stand at the spot that was once the center of a thriving ancient city.

Scientists have been excavating the ruins of Ur for more than a century. Only about 30 percent has been uncovered. Researchers continue to discover clues that help tell the story of the forgotten desert city and its mysterious pyramid.

Ancient engineers included square drainage holes in the walls of the ziggurat. The holes have helped protect the structure from water damage for thousands of years.

The Ziggurat of Ur is part of the Ahwar of Southern Iraq, an area listed in 2016 as a UNESCO World Heritage Site. This organization works to protect unique historical and cultural sites considered important to the entire world. Studies report the mud bricks of the ziggurat are threatened by **erosion** from winds and sand, as well as salt seeping in from the groundwater. The same is true of the Royal Cemetery and the rebuilt city of Babylon.

Conflict in the region also poses a danger to these important sites. Not only can structures be damaged, the funding necessary to maintain and repair them is not always available during times of war.

Heritage sites are always at risk during times of conflict. The Gulf War in the 1990s and the invasion of Iraq in the early 2000s led not only to damage but to looting of museums and historical archives. In addition, from 2014 to 2017, the ***terrorist*** *group called the Islamic State, or ISIS, destroyed mosques and shrines that it decided did not meet its strict interpretation of their religious views.*

GLOSSARY

afterlife (AF-ter-lyfe) Life that is believed to begin after death

archaeologists (ahr-kee-AH-luh-juhsts) Scientists who study the distant past by digging up things that people made, used, and left behind

artifacts (AHR-tuh-fakts) Objects made and used by humans in the past, including tools and weapons

carnelian (kahr-NEEL-yuhn) A brownish-red mineral often used as a semiprecious stone

civilizations (siv-uh-li-ZAY-shuhnz) Groups of people with their own language and way of life

compensating (KOM-puhn-say-ting) Making up for loss, damage, or injury, often by paying money

cuneiform (kyoo-NEE-uh-form) An ancient system of writing used in the Middle East, consisting of wedge-shaped characters often carved into soft clay tablets

erosion (i-ROH-zhuhn) The wearing away of Earth's crust by wind, water, or ice

excavate (EK-skuh-vayt) To dig up or uncover

facade (fuh-SAHD) The face or front of a building

inscribed (in-SKRYBD) Marked or carved with characters

irrigation (eer-uh-GAY-shuhn) The practice of supplying water to crops by guiding it through channels and pipes

lapis lazuli (LA-puhs LA-zuh-lee) A semiprecious stone that has a rich blue color

merchant (MUR-chuhnt) Someone who buys and sells goods and services

ornate (awr-NEYT) Having elaborate decorations or complex patterns

restoration (ress-tuh-RAY-shuhn) The act of returning something to its original condition

sacrifice (SAK-ruh-fyse) A religious act of killing a person or offering a valuable possession to a god or divine figure

terraced (TER-isd) Formed from a series of raised platforms with sloping sides

terrorist (TERR-er-rist) A person who uses fear and unlawful violence to achieve political or religious goals

tiers (teerz) Rows or layers placed one above the other

INDEX

QUESTIONS AFTER READING

1. The Ziggurat of Ur is located on land that is now the country of _____.
   a. Euphrates
   b. Iraq
   c. Mesopotamia

2. The city of Ur was abandoned because of ______.
   a. Queen Puabi's rule
   b. violence and war
   c. a changing landscape

3. At the very top of the Ziggurat of Ur was a ______.
   a. temple
   b. garden
   c. tomb

4. The ziggurat's bricks were made mostly of ______.
   a. carnelian b. mud c. grain

5. People used the Ziggurat of Ur for ______ purposes.
   a. practical
   b. spiritual
   c. both a and b

Answers: 1. b, 2. c, 3. a, 4. b, 5. c

ABOUT THE AUTHOR

Murray "Oak" Tapeta was born in a toilet-less cabin in Montana. Growing up in the great outdoors, he learned to love trees. He got the nickname "Oak" after climbing to the top of an oak tree when he was only three years old. Oak loves to read and write. He has written a number of books about fascinating, terrible, and gruesome events from the distant past. He prefers spending time in the wilderness with his dog, Birchy.

Author: Murray "Oak" Tapeta

Editor: Kathy Middleton

Proofreader: Crystal Sikkens

Design: Samara Parent and Kathy Walsh

Production coordinator: Candice Campbell

IMAGE CREDITS

Alamy: ©Photo12/Ann Ronan Picture Library: p 10-11;

Shutterstock: ©Mohammed_Al_Ali, p 6 (bottom left), p 27 (bottom); ©John Wreford: p 12 (bottom); ©Ariya Stock: p 21 (bottom); ©Focus and Blur: p 25 (top)

Wikimedia Commons: Public Domain: p 8-9 (bottom); ©Mike Peel (www.mikepeel.net): p 14 (bottom); ©Nic McPhee from Morris, Minnesota, USA: p 19 (bottom); ©Internet Archive Book Images: p 20; ©Dosseman: p 23 (bottom)

All other images from Shutterstock

Crabtree Publishing

crabtreebooks.com 800-387-7650

In Canada: We acknowledge the financial support of the Government of Canada through the Canada Book Fund for our publishing activities.

Hardcover 978-1-0398-7285-1
Paperback 978-1-0398-7343-8
Ebook (pdf) 978-1-0398-7398-8
Epub 978-1-0398-7447-3

Published in Canada
Crabtree Publishing
616 Welland Avenue
St. Catharines, Ontario
L2M 5V6

Published in the United States
Crabtree Publishing
347 Fifth Avenue
Suite 1402-145
New York, New York, 10016

Library and Archives Canada Cataloguing in Publication
Available at Library and Archives Canada

Library of Congress Cataloging-in-Publication Data
Available at the Library of Congress

Printed in the U.S.A./CP052026